FASHION IN THE TIME OF JANE AUSTEN

Sarah Jane Downing

SHIRE PUBLICATIONS

Published in Great Britain in 2011 by Shire Publications Ltd, Midland House, West Way, Botley, Oxford OX2 0PH, United Kingdom.
44-02 23rd Street, Suite 219, Long Island City, NY 11101, USA.

E-mail: shire@shirebooks.co.uk   www.shirebooks.co.uk

Shire Library no. 583   •   ISBN-13: 978 0 74780 767 4

Sarah Jane Downing has asserted her right under the Copyright, Designs and Patents Act, 1988, to be identified as the author of this book.

Designed by Tony Truscott
Printed in China through Worldprint Ltd.

11 12 13 14 15   12 11 10 9 8 7 6 5 4 3

COVER IMAGE
Two Strings to her Bow, by John Pettie (1887).

TITLE PAGE IMAGE
Afternoon dress, 1812.

CONTENTS PAGE IMAGE
Jerry in Training for a Swell (*Life in London* by Pierce Egan, 1822). Cut and fit were everything even if a corset like the one discarded on the floor was necessary. '*Clothes maketh the man*' and already London tailors were renowned for their incredible skill in creating a gentleman.

ACKNOWLEDGEMENTS
Illustrations are acknowledged as follows:
Bridgeman Art Library, cover and pages 4, 11 (lower), 12, 22, 28, 30, 32, 36, 46 and 60; Alison J. Carter, Senior Keeper of Art & Design, Hampshire County Council Museums and Archives Service, pages 21 and 48 (upper); Cora Ginsburg LLC, page 45; Victor Hassall, Bonhams, page 57 (lower); Michelle Hyde, page 14 (upper right) and 39 (lower); The Jane Austen Memorial Trust, pages 53, and 58 (lower); Eleanor Keene of Bonhams, page 24 and 40 (lower); Musée Carnavalet, page 6 (upper); and Simon Wheeler (Wheeler Estate), page 62 (upper).

The Fashion Museum at Bath has been wonderful in its kind support for this book, as has The Jane Austen Memorial Trust, which loaned the photographs of Jane's white muslin scarf, page 53 and the topaz crosses that belonged to Jane and Cassandra, page 58 (bottom).

Finally, my heartfelt thanks to my sister Emma, my parents, especially my mother for her French translations, Sacha and David, and to those fabulous people at Shire Publications, especially Nick Wright and Russell Butcher.

CONTENTS

THE AGE OF ELEGANCE

THE WORLD was on the brink of revolution when Jane Austen was born on 16 December 1775. The battle for American Independence heralded an era marked by decades of war and conflict as the old order was swept away in an explosion of radical ideas and technological innovations. As the modern era loomed on the horizon, propelled by capitalism and industrialisation, fashion became the barometer of change. Looking for the first time beyond the decorative, it embodied the philosophical, the political and the practical issues of the day. For the first time England not only revolutionised style, but with industrialisation it revolutionised the process to produce it.

It was an era of contradiction immortalised by Jane Austen, who adeptly used the newfound diversity of fashion to enliven her characters: Wickham's military splendour, Mr Darcy's understated elegance, and Miss Tilney's romantic fixation with white muslin. They are characterised by their dress but rarely do they speak of it; unless they are one of Austen's sillier characters, they maintain the good taste and decorum of the times, which held that it was poor manners to impose conversation about such footling matters upon company. It was within her private correspondence with her beloved sister Cassandra that she discussed such fripperies as her plans for new bonnet trimmings and the successful reception received by her black velvet cap.

Jane was essentially of the gentry, very aware of the correct way to behave but not necessarily with an income large enough to make it happen easily. Taste and poise should come naturally to a lady, and it was an indictment of a lack of breeding to be worried about looking correct. The drawing room tensions of fashion and faux pas that she so beautifully illustrated were the furthermost ripples of the revolutions that were changing the world.

The impenetrable class order that had held strong since time immemorial was gradually being breached by a budding generation of increasingly wealthy industrialists, entrepreneurs and merchants who were making their own place in society through their ideas and innovations. Their impact was huge, not only in the foundation of the textiles industry and

Opposite:
The Cloakroom, Clifton Assembly Rooms (Rolinda Sharples, 1817–18). Polite society was increasingly diverse and exciting – one lady is helped with the removal of her outside shoes, but the others are more interested in the eligible bachelors.

5

Ah! What Relics!!! Oh! What a Foolish New Fashion... (engraved by Chataîgnier 1797). There was a radical contrast between the old and new fashions as the exaggerated display of hereditary privilege was exchanged for a modern mix of style and practicality.

Below: *The Advertisement For a Wife* (*The Third Tour of Dr. Syntax*, Rowlandson, c. 1821). There was huge competition for any eligible bachelor so it was essential to be as beautiful and fashionable as possible.

international trade, but in their eagerness to display their newly gentrified status with all the trappings of a country estate.

Fashions had tended to originate at the French Court, transferring to England through royal circles, but throughout the revolutionary years and the Napoleonic wars the typical route for fashions and fabrics coming from France was severed. This coincided with increasing trade with India, which imported fine muslins, cashmere shawls and the raw cotton to be processed by the rapidly growing numbers of mills appearing across the north of England. In France muslins were fashionably democratic for their affordability but in England they were doubly so, as many people became wealthy from cotton and were amongst the first to attain social mobility.

Yorkshire cotton factory child workers, c. 1814. Democratic cottons represented a new egalitarian age for some, but many others lost their independence when they were forced to exchange their cottage industries for the oppressive factory system.

Jane was fourteen in the year the Bastille was stormed marking the beginning of the period of turbulence that would launch democracy as a new force in the world. She had a direct link with the tragedies of the Revolution through her cousin Eliza de Feuillide, who had been married to the Comte de Feuillide before marrying Jane's brother in 1797. Eliza was in England in February 1794 when she heard that her husband had met *la guillotine*, news that would make the horror of the Revolution shockingly real to all the Austen family.

The Angler's Repast (George Morland, c. 1789). Rousseau's ideas about nature became very influential, and as the closest acceptable thing to nature, the English country gentleman unexpectedly found himself a style icon.

A very rare fashion plate from a dressmaker's journal of 1817, giving an embroidery pattern as well as fashions for the upcoming season that would be recreated to order for customers.

Costume Parisien.

Mois de Juin.

'Morning Dresses' (*The Gallery of Fashion*, April 1797). Heideloff was a miniaturist in Paris before the Terror and his beautiful illustrations for *The Gallery of Fashion* revolutionised the fashion press.

Before the Revolution Eliza had enjoyed an illustrious lifestyle in France with the Comte, and frequently wrote to tell her cousins of visiting Marie Antoinette at Trianon, including full details of the queen's gowns. Jane enjoyed her keen and witty observations, later using Eliza as inspiration for her novel *Lady Susan*. Marie Antoinette had a major role in changing fashion away from the tightly corseted ornate gowns with vast skirts over pannier hoops, which she reputedly loathed wearing, to

8

the simpler *style à l'anglaise*. Rousseau's love affair with the English political system also encouraged the adoption of English fashions, as their studied casualness was regarded as elegantly democratic.

Having been forced to flee from the Terror, many of Paris' finest modistes and their clients arrived in London and quickly it became the new fashion capital. Amongst them was Nicolaus Wilhelm Von Heideloff who founded *The Gallery of Fashion* in 1794; its beautiful illustrations were inspirational and the fashion press soon took over as the premier conduit for fashion intelligence, encouraging a faster turnover of more diverse styles. Prior to that, fashions were rather charmingly delivered from Paris to the Courts of Europe by *les grands courriers de la mode*, life-size mannequin messengers dressed in every detail of the latest fashions, which would be tried on and taken apart so that patterns could be taken from them.

Women who participated in London society or who visited the fashionable centres were prevailed upon to relay every scrap of detail about the outfits of the most fashionable ladies they had seen. Like Mrs Gardiner in *Pride and Prejudice*, whose first duty upon arriving at the Bennet household was to 'distribute her presents and describe the latest fashions', they were undoubtedly pleased to do so with a sense of one-upmanship – but probably only after they had already commissioned their own dressmakers to start work!

Jane Austen herself regularly included fashion news in her letters when she was in Bath or London: 'I am amused by the present style of female dress; – the coloured petticoats with braces over the white Spencers & enormous Bonnets upon the full stretch, are quite entertaining. It seems to me a more marked change than one has lately seen.'

With improved awareness of fashion it was increasingly important for young ladies to be fashionable as well as beautiful and well dressed. This important period marked the transition away from the old wide hooped silhouette, which remained reserved strictly for wearing at Court, to the modern vertical silhouette. For some years gowns were becoming narrower, with a rising

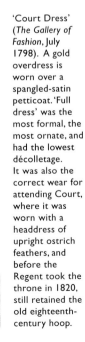

'Court Dress' (*The Gallery of Fashion*, July 1798). A gold overdress is worn over a spangled-satin petticoat. 'Full dress' was the most formal, the most ornate, and had the lowest décolletage. It was also the correct wear for attending Court, where it was worn with a headdress of upright ostrich feathers, and before the Regent took the throne in 1820, still retained the old eighteenth-century hoop.

9

Mr and Mrs Hallett (after Thomas Gainsborough, 1785). Although Mr Hallett is not as fashionable as his wife, with her Buffon and picture hat she gives a beautiful depiction of the softer style à l'anglaise.

waistline, and simpler, often taking inspiration from the masculine redingote or greatcoat. A puff of muslin known as a 'Buffon' gave modesty to the décolletage and brought interest upwards to the face, which was framed prettily by a coiffure of natural curls and topped by a large picture hat.

Jane was making her debut at the Basingstoke assemblies in 1792 just as fashions were becoming more changeable and responsive to what was going on in the world. Already an accomplished

writer, having just completed *A History of England by a Partial, Prejudiced and Ignorant Historian*, she was probably still more aware of other people's fashions than her own.

Although film adaptations of Jane's books usually set the costumes in the 1800s, her initial drafts of the novels that later became *Pride and Prejudice, Sense and Sensibility*, and *Northanger Abbey* were written between 1795 and 1798 and would have been set in the clothes of the day, if only in her imagination.

Jane has been criticised for writing little about the tremendous events that marked her era, but it was considered unseemly for ladies to discuss such matters. Yet, they arrived nonetheless, translated into garments and

Journal des Dames (1790). Inspired by the English redingote, the dress of lavender grey silk is worn over a white muslin petticoat with a Buffon and blue scarf crossed and tied as a sash.

details of fashion. The delicate muslins that defined the era were born of the French Revolution, the neoclassical details were inspired by the political desire to emulate the democratic republics of the ancient world, and the military flourishes a response to the protracted period of war in which proportionately more British servicemen died than during the First World War. Fashion's dramatic response was to make women reed-slender, their waistlines clinging to their bosoms as though for comfort, their silhouette sleek and etiolated, whilst male fashions took on the lean and statuesque lines of a Grecian hero or Olympiad.

Jane's era was defined by the people who were willing

Evening full dress (*La Belle Assemblée*, January 1810). Fashions became undeniably sexy, foretelling those that would appear at the time of the First World War.

Below left: The *Rice Portrait* (Ozias Humphry, c.1792–3), thought by some to be of a young Jane Austen, was originally held within the Austen-Knight family collection.

to take their voice and speak out, and those who would use their ideas and talents to make a life for themselves as she herself did. Jane's works seem very conventional from a twenty-first-century perspective, as do the fashions, but taking the timeframe of Jane's major writing period from 1791 to her death in 1817, this book will show that it is a unique moment in fashion unequalled in its daring nudity, cropped hair and masculine styling until the jazz age nearly a century later.

In defiance of the French Revolution, both men and women wore their hair *à la Victime*, with the front brought forward in a tousled fringe; this was later modified as the Titus coiffure.

THE RISE OF ENGLISH FASHION

FOR MALE FASHION it was the 'battle between broadcloth and silk' as Balzac had termed it in 1798, and the broadcloth had triumphed. Gone were the old prim white stockings and buckle shoes of the eighteenth century; the mannered ennui of pretty silks and vile gossip was overtaken by young men who stepped in with fresh air clinging to their clothes and mud spattered on their boots. Their style and virility spoke of a bolder, faster life more natural in the fresh air of the countryside. Casual yet suave, the riding coat or redingote became the central piece of the male wardrobe. It could be single- or double-breasted, either tapering towards the back in the style of a morning coat (which remained the more formal), or the sporty square 'cut-in' coat with the front amputated below the waist to leave only tails at the back. This became the norm for informal 'undress' after 1810 and was, with longer tails, the style preferred by the Dandies.

Where neckcloths became hugely important, shirts were not regarded as such and were one of the sewing tasks assigned to female relatives rather than professional tailors. In November 1800 Jane rushed to complete a batch for her brother: 'I have heard from Charles, and am to send his shirts by half-dozens as they are finished; one set will go next week. The "Endymion" is now waiting only for orders, but may wait for them perhaps a month'. In *Mansfield Park* Fanny Price works diligently to ensure that her brother's linen is ready when he goes to sea, and in *Northanger Abbey* Catherine Morland is supposed to be making cravats for her brother but finds other activities far more interesting.

Breeches, the staple of the eighteenth-century wardrobe, were increasingly neglected in favour of more comfortable sporting wear. As they made an aristocratic statement they were sidelined into formal 'full dress' and remained the only garment acceptable at Court, at the smartest Pleasure Gardens, and also the prestigious Almack's Club.

The name derived from the character from *commedia dell'arte*, the 'Pantalon' or pantaloons became the forerunner to trousers. Pantaloons were considered so worryingly revolutionary that in 1807 the Russian Tsar had

Opposite:
Portrait of Pierre Seriziat (Jacques Louis David, 1795). The cut-away redingote, form-hugging suede buckskins, top boots, tall hat and pristine neckcloth spoke of a bolder, faster lifestyle more natural in the fresh air of the countryside.

13

Right: *Journal des Dames 1790.* The redingote at the beginning of its evolution; worn in bold striped silk with breeches and buckle shoes, it still retains the old refined formality.

Far right: *Young Gentleman on the Grand Tour 1812.* The redingote having reached its Regency ideal; the practical lines and practical fabrics equipped the gentleman for a new era of action.

troops set up roadblocks to examine travellers' leg wear, and anyone discovered wearing them had their pantaloons forcibly cut off at the knees. Related to the tight buckskin breeches worn for riding by English gentlemen since the mid-eighteenth century, they were frequently made of a semi-stretch fabric like stockinette or were bias cut, the skin-tight pantaloons giving the virile look of a classical statue. Worn with knee-length half boots or Hessians, pantaloons came to mid-calf and were tied with ribbons at the sides.

Boots were the democratic ideal, taken up by the Parisian *bon ton*; the English boot reigned supreme for its superior quality and fit. The most fashionable were the 'top-boot': worn with breeches and buckskins and looking like a riding boot, they were black knee-length leather with a light coloured top. Worn with pantaloons and inspired by the uniform boots worn by the Hussars, Hessians had a high curved front reaching just below the knee where the 'V' shaped notch was decorated with a hanging gold tassel, or silver for mourning. Also to be worn with pantaloons, Hussar boots

Le Bon Genre, c. 1810. Double-breasted waistcoats with shawl collars became popular in the 1790s and remained so into the second decade of the nineteenth century. Tied at mid-calf, pantaloons could be worn as they are here with striped stockings and modern lace up shoes, or with boots.

Tom and Jerry Sporting a Toe among the Corinthians at Almacks (*Life in London* by Pierce Egan, 1822). Nothing less than formal 'full dress' was acceptable at the prestigious Almack's Club, as the Duke of Wellington discovered to his chagrin when even he was turned away for wearing trousers in 1814.

or 'buskins' resembled short calf-length Hessians but without the tassel. After 1819 the Wellington boot was added to the available repertoire – named for the Duke, they were very similar to the top-boot but without the coloured turnover.

Previously, hats had been confined to the tricorne model, but even though highwaymen had managed, they were impractical for riding to hounds as they were apt to fly off at high speeds. A high crown was useful (if scant) protection against head injuries, and also had a nice status look. The receding brim and growing crown which combined in the round hat eventually grew into the top hat.

An Evening at Frascati, 1809. For Court or evening wear the opera hat or cocked hat resembled the military bicorne (see gentleman background left). It was worn with the points to front and back like Nelson rather than side-to-side like Napoleon. It was a *chapeau bras*, most frequently tucked under the arm rather than worn.

15

This full dress evening gown with asymmetrical Grecian style tunic from 1811 shows that the romance with Neo-classicism continued unabated.

The divergence of the lives of men and women was marked entirely by their clothes: when they both wore silk and lace and habituated the same drawing rooms, they shared courtly love or gossipy intrigue. With the advent of the nineteenth century, if they weren't at war or at sea, gentlemen were eyeing horses at Tattersall's, racing curricles, or were at their club. The only time they would really interact with women was in the evenings at the theatre, opera, Pleasure Gardens, or dancing, where formal full dress of the old order was required.

Although women's styles were simpler there were still the demarcations of 'full dress', 'half dress' and 'undress' that ruled the propriety of fashion, and English etiquette was set almost like a trap to pull rank on newly moneyed arrivistes even if fashions were more democratic. 'Undress' or *déshabillé* referred to simpler gowns worn at home in the morning, often with a cap. Made of warmer, more practical materials, they would often be looser and more comfortable for sitting writing letters, sewing or reading. 'Half dress' covered smarter more formal ensembles for activities such as afternoon promenades, visiting, or even trips to the opera. 'Full dress' was the most formal, the most ornate, and had the lowest décolletage. Worn for balls, Almack's, the premier Pleasure Gardens, and the most luscious parties, it was also the correct wear for attending Court, where it was worn with a headdress of upright ostrich feathers.

Whereas gentlemen's clothes changed to reflect their changed lifestyle, the most significant changes for women were to the silhouette. Although in Paris the high-waisted silhouette was lauded as the apex of the refinement of classical antiquity, in England the 'waist-less gown' was frequently greeted as an abomination especially by male commentators —as in the satirical song, *Shepherds, I Have Lost My Waist*:

'Morning Dress' (*La Belle Assemblée*, 1814). Domestic bliss: mother and baby in matching white ruffles. Her cap is trimmed with pink ribbon, and her bodice has pink 'braces' that cup the bosom giving extra support.

Shepherds, I have lost my waist,
Have you seen my body?
Sacrificed to modern taste,
I'm quite a hoddy-doddy!
For fashion I that part forsook
Where sages place the belly;
'Tis gone – and I have not a nook
For cheesecake, tart or jelly.
Never shall I see it more,
Till common sense returning,
My body to my legs restore,
Then I shall cease from mourning.
Folly and fashion do prevail
To such extremes upon the fair
A woman's only top and tail,
The body's banish'd God knows where!

Wiener Moden,
1816. A long-
sleeved evening
gown of white
gauze with pink
satin roses and
a striped satin
petticoat worn
with pink shoes
and white gloves.

Fashionable ladies could not have paid much attention, as the waist remained high until the mid-1820s, with only a brief hiatus whilst Napoleon excluded England from trade with Europe. The first 'Grecian' gowns were simple shifts of muslin with practically no shape except that given by a ribbon tied beneath the bosom. It was a style most suited to the young and slender, and although it did not carry the political significance held in France, the freedom and comfort of a light gown worn with little underpinning and flat slippers must have been a relief that many women were unwilling to give up.

Gowns were décolleté even for day when the neckline might be 'V'-shaped or square with a tucker. The round gown had bodice and skirt joined with a seam round the waistline, whereas open gowns were split at the front – as they had been for much of the eighteenth century – allowing an underskirt of contrasting colour or fabric to show.

'Half Dress'
(Ackermann's
Repository, 1816).
Half dress of pink
and white striped
percale with
Mameluke sleeves,
knots of green
ribbon and white
ruchings. After
1810 skirts were
more frequently
shorter with
decorative details
around the hem.

17

The petticoat was a dress worn beneath the robe or open gown as another layer of formal garment rather than underwear. The petticoat provided a convenient extra layer that could be used to give a contrast or depth of colour allowing the outer dress to be gossamer thin. A modern variation appearing at the turn of the century was the tunic dress, extremely popular for its Greco-Roman overtones; it had a tunic often in a contrasting colour bordered in gold, worn asymmetrically over a plain dress.

It could also allow the richer fabric of the outer dress to be tucked out of the way when walking through muddy lanes without the danger of showing an indecent ankle. But even this was not without criticism as Elizabeth Bennet found when she arrived at Netherfield to visit her sister after a three-mile cross-country walk. Miss Bingley couldn't wait to say: 'I hope you saw her petticoat, six inches deep in mud, I am absolutely certain; and the gown which had been let down to hide it not doing its office.' Older dresses were often recycled as petticoats, as Jane Austen mentions in a letter in December 1798.

Trains became a feature of gowns for day and evening wear in 1800 as Oliver Goldsmith notes:

'Evening Dress' (*Ackermann's Repository*, October 1817). Beautiful evening dress with tiers of Vandyked lace and rouleau bound with strings of pearls.

As a lady's quality or fashion was once determined here by the circumference of her hoop, both are now measured by the length of her tail. Women of moderate fortunes are contented with tails moderately long but ladies of true taste and distinction set no bounds to their ambition in this particular.

Men were often less enthusiastic, complaining of tripping over them, but many gowns had a method of allowing the train to be pulled up out of the way like those of Catherine and Isabella Thorpe, who 'pinned up each other's train for the dance' when they were dancing at the assembly rooms in *Northanger Abbey*.

It is impossible to underestimate how important dancing was to the Regency lady; there were so few opportunities to meet that eligible bachelor with ten thousand a year, and so much competition in the flooded marriage market that every ball or assembly had to be approached strategically with the perfect gown as the most important element.

Just as riding costume offered men a freedom of cut that was so desirable that it was translated into ordinary wear, it did the same for women. Providing a more practical yet still fashionable ensemble, the riding habit frequently enjoyed male styling, taking its

A Group of Waltzers, 1817. Dancing was a wonderful opportunity for a young lady to display her beauty and grace; it also offered a very rare chance for her to speak to a beau without being overheard by her ever-present chaperone.

The Squire's Door (after George Morland, c. 1790). A stylish riding habit with wide lapels and caped shoulders is based on a gentleman's greatcoat. Her hat echoes the new taller masculine styles as worn by the gentleman in the background.

19

Right: *La Belle Assemblée* (February 1813). The caption read: 'A stone coloured habit, trimmed round the body with swansdown, and ornamented entirely across the bosom with a thick row of rich silk braiding to correspond ... Large bear or seal skin muff; stone coloured kid gloves, and black kid sandals.'

Far right: 'Spencer' (*Ackermann's Repository*, 1817). For an English winter – indeed, many days in an English summer – a muslin gown would have been too cold and the Spencer was readily taken up for warmth, as Jane notes in June 1808: 'My kerseymere Spencer is quite the comfort of our Evening walks.'

inspiration from the gentleman's greatcoat towards the end of the eighteenth century, and sporting military braid at the beginning of the nineteenth. Usually made from woollen, or in summer linen fabrics, it became popular for travelling and more energetic activities. Brides often chose a new riding habit as their going-away outfit. In *Emma*, Jane Fairfax is wearing hers for a boat trip at Weymouth when she is nearly 'dashed into the sea' only to be saved by Mr Dixon who 'with the greatest presence of mind, caught hold of her habit'.

From the late 1790s, for daywear, redingotes, pelisses, and riding habits, sleeves for both men and women were very long, fitted to the wrist and covering the back of the hand to the top of the thumb. For evening 'full dress' the short puffed sleeve reigned supreme until 1807 when *La Belle Assemblée* announced: 'the long sleeve is very generally introduced in evening dress but is ever composed of the clearest materials; sometimes of lace, patent or spider-net, and embroidered book muslin.' Even so, the accepted formal short sleeve was so established that in 1814 Jane wrote:

> I wear my gauze gown today long sleeves & all; I shall see how they succeed, but as yet I have no reason to suppose long sleeves are allowable. Mrs. Tilson has long sleeves too, & she assured me that they are worn in the evening by many. I was glad to hear this.

She wrote in another letter later the same year from London, 'long sleeves appear universal, even as Dress.'

The Spencer became the most fashionable solution for keeping warm, remaining in style until the second decade of the nineteenth century. It was named after Lord Spencer who when he singed his coat tails whilst warming himself in front of the fire removed the tails and wore the coat without! It translated to women's wear, coming into fashion in the 1790s as a short fitted jacket only as long as the bodice, usually with long fitted sleeves and high collar. Typically made of woollen cloth, or possibly silk or velvet, it was almost always a strong colour, in contrast to the white skirt of the gown beneath, and had the added advantage of complementing the lines of the gown.

Another development of the late 1790s was the pelisse. Like a coat, it was an over garment that could be added for warmth on cold days, cut with a high waist and skirt to follow the line of the gown it was worn with. It had the potential for glamour as Fanny Price found in *Mansfield Park* when, during a visit to Portsmouth, judgment was passed on hers – 'she neither played on the pianoforte nor wore fine pelisses' – and she was found less than socially desirable.

The pelisse came into its own as gowns narrowed after the turn of the century partly because it complemented the leaner line, and partly because the thin muslin gowns with scant underwear were leaving ladies positively chilled. The pelisse was a welcome outer layer for warmth and being a heavier fabric – velvet or wool in the colder months, and sarsenet or silks in summer – it provided a new scope for decoration.

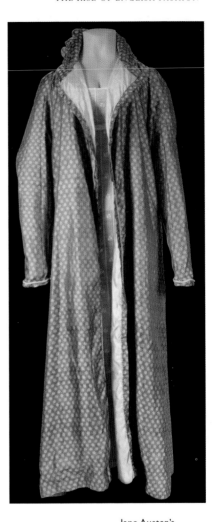

Jane Austen's pelisse, c. 1814. Made in twill weave silk with a repeat design of oak leaves, it would suggest that she was quite tall and slender at approximately 5 feet 7 inches, with a 30–32-inch bust, making her a modern UK size 6 or US size 2.

A FINE ROMANCE

ONCE THE VIOLENT upheavals of the Revolutionary era had been banished to memory, concepts of nation began to change in favour of a more sensitive relationship with history. Both the French and Industrial revolutions had precipitated a headlong dash into a 'better' future against a growing dissatisfaction with the present. For the first time tradition began to be appreciated as something other than simply the lot of the unfashionable or uninitiated. Both England and France turned to the past for inspiration, first in literature, then dress, furnishings and architecture, in a romance with history that would last well into the Victorian era.

The rise of the novel led by Sir Walter Scott offered Scotland as a muse and as a way of contemplating rebellion and revolution at a safe distance. A version of 'trouses' or 'trews' had been worn for centuries by Highlanders, especially for riding. They were worn by the Scottish nobles of the Jacobite Rising in 1745 when they tried to restore the Stuarts to the throne, and after the defeat at Culloden by Charles Edward Stuart the 'Young Pretender' as he made his sad retreat, sailing to France in 'a short coat of coarse, black frieze, tartan trews, and over them a belted plaid'. The Jacobites had been all but forgotten apart from their sartorial impact, which led to a ban on wearing tartan, lasting thirty-five years.

The old rebel Scotland also provided common ground in 1800 when Schiller's *Maria Stuart* fired imaginations with the tale of the brave, passionate and tragic Queen who had also lost her head. Ruffs and slashed sleeves appeared on both sides of the channel, and by 1820 had become so popular for day wear they were encroaching upon the evening. Aside from the odd ruff that was flung back from the décolletage in the style of Elizabeth I, generally the ruff brought necklines higher. Slashed sleeves were also of a suitable length to accommodate more detail, allowing for ruffs to appear at the wrists, and historical flourishes combined to create a new modesty after Waterloo.

It was as though after the turmoil of the war years there had to be a period of mourning to assess just what had been lost, and led by the literature

Opposite:
In romantic reverie: *Miss Lamont of Greenock* (by Sir Henry Raeburn, c. 1810–15)

23

Early nineteenth-century redingote of figured cream silk and a cream silk dress. Pale and interesting could also be pale and perfectly luxurious with lavish decorations of silk gauze with floral work and loop cord braiding with thread-covered beads.

Opposite (left): *Le Journal des Dames et des Modes Costumes Parisiens*, 1818. The black velvet hat gives a delightful historical hint of Mary Queen of Scots to a striking red evening gown.

Opposite (right): *Le Journal des Dames et des Modes Costumes Parisiens*, 1821. Taking the Tudor vogue to the extreme, this gown of white tulle with matching bonnet has ruffs at collar, shoulder, wrist and hem.

of the age things took on a decidedly Gothic melancholy. Lord Byron and many of the other Romantic poets took on an air of the 'blighted being' overtly displaying their sensitivity as an ethereal mark of 'otherness'.

Ladies were so committed to figure-revealing styles that little was worn with their scanty muslin gowns even in winter, giving rise to an increase in the incidence of consumption, so doctors thought, who dubbed it the 'muslin disease'. Consumption or tuberculosis was rife, affecting all classes; it drained

vitality from the soul and roses from the cheeks leaving its victims frail and wan. One folkloric belief was that the consumptive was forced to spend all night at fairy revels leaving them weak by day, barely able to rise from an elegantly proportioned daybed whilst gradually fading away to the other side. If a lady wasn't fortunate enough to suffer from such a glamorous illness, she could feign going 'into decline'. The desirable fragile consumptive look was simulated by drinking vinegar and dropping belladonna into their eyes,

The Fair Spirit, beautiful and delicate in ethereal white, visits Lord Byron, far more substantial but no less romantic in voluminous cloak, Hussar boots, with his signature open collar, considered very risqué in the day of the starched neckcloth.

creating a deathly pallor punctuated only by wild dark eyes. *La Belle Assemblée* wrote in 1806: 'wrap them in elegant robes of light impalpable ether', and where once white was the sheer and semi-nude drapery of a Grecian statue, Gothic white was an ethereal shroud of multilayered muslin and moonlight.

Women had been left on the sidelines as their world was changed around them. As Jane Austen's works make painfully clear, there was only one real prospect for a woman to lead a full and happy life and that was by making a successful marriage, but with so many men lost to the Napoleonic wars decent marriage prospects were scarce. With scant hope of a tantalising proposal, it is no

White muslin dresses, 1795. Muslins were wonderfully modern, and not only in the ideas they represented; the practicality of soft washable fabrics that would drape beautifully without an underlying structure was revolutionary. White was the colour of antiquity and the hallmark of elegance; moreover, it was more easily dressed and accessorised than other colours.

wonder that so many young women identified with the poetic 'blighted being', falling in love with the drama of love unrequited. A life of fragility hovering on the brink of dire illness epitomised the romantic ideal and sentimentality became the vogue with young ladies schooled in how to swoon or dissolve into tears in a suitably elegant and charming way.

Heroines like Emily in *The Mysteries of Udolpho* spent an inordinate amount of time wearing a white veil whilst being chased through romantic ruinous European landscapes by villainous relatives and unworthy suitors.

Jane Elizabeth Countess of Oxford (after John Hoppner, 1797). Being suited to the heart-fluttering, largely imaginary passions of innocent young girls, white was the colour of choice for the heroines of novels such as *The Mysteries of Udolpho* by one of Jane's contemporary authors, Ann Radcliffe.

In *Northanger Abbey* Catherine Morland and Eleanor Tilney are obsessed by the novel and Miss Tilney always wears white like Emily. In keeping with her semi-parody of the gothic novel form, white – especially white muslin – plays a pivotal role in the nascent relationship between Catherine and Henry Tilney, who is marked as sensitive and gallant by his understanding of muslins.

The simple democratic muslin had become the mainstay of fashion, and with the triumph of industrialisation, was affordable to everyone. Where once this was thought an advantage, by 1813 it was lamented that 'as to dress, no distinction exists between mistress and maid except that one wears a cap'. The gentry took a very dim view of lower-class women attempting to copy their fashions, as in *Mansfield Park* where the housekeeper is commended as she 'turned away two housemaids for wearing white gowns'.

The Gallery of Fashion, 1795. Edmund tells Fanny in *Mansfield Park*, 'a woman can never be too fine whilst she is all in white. No, I see no finery about you; nothing but what is perfectly proper. Your gown seems very pretty. I like these glossy spots. Has not Miss Crawford a gown something the same?'

BEAU BRUMMELL AND THE GREAT RENUNCIATION

J ANE MAKES little comment about men's apparel, but in the understated elegance she writes for Mr Darcy it is easy to see the hallmark of Beau Brummell. It is testament to the power of a prodigious personality that Beau Brummell, through his connection with the Regent, was able to influence such a profound change in dress almost single-handed. The genus of the idea – the English country gentleman's cut-away riding coat, tight pantaloons, tall boots and tall hat – had been batted back and forth from England to France for years but it was Beau Brummell who made it the *only* acceptable way for a fashionable gentleman to dress. Under his direction, the *style à l'anglaise* was drawn away from the discordant statement of the Revolution and into modernity, creating the ensemble that would be the basis of the male wardrobe for the next hundred years.

The Regency gentleman was no stranger to colour: combinations of black, white and sage green; purple, white and yellow; or blue, crimson and canary were all thought to be in good taste even with the addition of accessories in other colours. Beau Brummell encouraged a more subtle palette of a well-tailored dark cloth jacket, plain light waistcoat, tightly fitted light leg wear and freshly laundered starched linen. These hallmarks of sobriety were defined by taste and self-assured style rather than the rich overstated trappings of hereditary status.

Lord Byron wrote of George Beau Brummell as being the second most important man in Europe after Napoleon – placing himself as a modest third! This cannot have been very pleasing to the poor old Regent who reputedly felt himself a rather disappointing portly second in the fashion stakes, and compensated for his lack of personal glamour by constantly tweaking the details of the uniforms belonging to his regiments. Beau Brummell had been in the Prince of Wales' Regiment the 10th Hussars from 1794 to 1798, and being part of this most glamorous regiment can only have compounded his already fastidious approach to dress.

Applying classical principles of line and proportion along with subtle tonal shades, the silhouette was defined by its tailoring. Classical statues

Opposite:
Portrait of George 'Beau' Brummell (Robert Dighton, 1805). George Beau Brummell used subtlety to frame his ego with an arrogant insouciance, which was doggedly emulated by his followers – including his 'fat friend' the Prince Regent.

Portrait of Joseph-Antoine de Nogent (Jean Auguste Dominique Ingres, 1815). Beau Brummell introduced a subtle palette but it was often worn with a sense of drama. It was reputed that some gentlemen soaked their pale suede buckskins so they would shrink to fit giving a striking impression of nudity.

showed men tall, lean limbed, broad shouldered and heroic. They also often showed them unclothed, so naturally a trouser to define a strong well-turned leg would be bias cut and skin-tight in a light neutral shade almost the colour of flesh. For those with less than heroic proportions, the art of the tailor sculpted them anew from cloth, padding puny shoulders and arms, puffing out sunken chests and corseting well-fed stomachs. Even a scraggy or twisted leg could be made more 'poetic' by judicious padding but, as the cavalry officer who wrote *The Whole Art of Dress* advised, 'in which cases a slight

Hamburger Journal der Moden und Eleganz, 1802. About Tom Lefroy with whom she had a flirtation, Jane wrote to Cassandra, 'he has but one fault, which time will, I trust, entirely remove – it is that his morning coat is a great deal too light.'

Brummell as a Young Man (engraved by J. Cooke). Tying the perfect cravat could take hours, and many attempts, each starched neckcloth discarded if it did not tie correctly the first time. Captain Jesse saw Brummell's valet 'coming downstairs one day with a quantity of tumbled neckcloths under his arm, and being interrogated on the subject, [he] solemnly replied "Oh, they are our failures."'

degree of stuffing is absolutely requisite, but the greatest care and circumspection should be used.'

The dandy was not the decorated fop of the eighteenth century, but exemplary of modern man informed by classicism and the heroic model set by Nelson and Wellington. Cut and fit were everything, creating a codified language for those in the know. Brummell's credo was, 'If John Bull turns to look after you, you are not well dressed'. Wealth was whispered in the skill of the tailor, not the precious fabrics, and class was implied by the hauteur given by a correctly tied cravat that held the head high causing movement to be limited and precise. In his biography of Brummell, Captain Jesse recalls:

The collar which was always fixed to his shirt, was so large that, before being folded down, it completely hid his head and face, and the white neckcloth was at least a foot in height. The first *coup d'archet* was made with the shirt collar, which he folded down to its proper size; and Brummell then standing before the glass, with his chin poked up to the ceiling, by the gentle and gradual declension of his lower jaw, creased the cravat to reasonable dimensions, the form of each succeeding crease being perfected with the shirt which he had just discarded.

Portrait of Colonel Evgraf V. Davydov (Orest Adamovich Kiprensky, 1809). The dashing uniforms of the Prussian Hussars were a huge influence on the uniforms designed for the British military.

Brummell's dress ethos was the first step in social mobility allowing for those like Pen's father in Thackeray's *Pendennis* to slip up a class from moneyed trade to the middle class of minor gentleman. Otherwise social mobility was through the Navy where there were opportunities to gain wealth from the 'prize money' divvied up between the crew when an enemy ship was captured, or the Army, where officers were invited to mix with the best families in England and had unprecedented opportunities to make money in foreign lands.

A Gentleman's Toilet (Lewis Marks, 1800). Women were not the only ones to wear falsies; men resortd to their own artifice, and 'false curves' were popular to make a puny leg more 'poetic'.

With two brothers serving, Jane's affiliation lay strongly with the Navy, who were rapidly redeeming their seamy reputations through victory and heroism. With the Navy protecting England with an 'impenetrable wooden wall', the militia were left to keep order within. Aside from a few locally contained riots there was not too much to do, and the militia quite swiftly earned a reputation for being more interested in drilling and parties than any kind of action.

Where Naval uniforms in trusty blue were generally still cut from a pattern designed in the 1780s, the glamorous bright red uniforms of the militia were up to date, with tightly fitted trousers, short jackets and hessian boots. The Navy needed more than eight hundred crew for each warship and thousands of men were far away at the front line, whereas the men in the militia (like Wickham) were at home partying and using their military splendour to turn young girls' heads, especially those rather superficial like Lydia Bennet. Older women were not immune, however, as Jane wrote for Mrs Bennet:
'I remember the time when I liked a red coat myself very well...

Second Dragoons 1812. This soldier's tall shako hat is attached to his jacket by a lanyard to avoid it being lost in battle and his sabretache hanging behind his knee would be more easily accessible when on horseback. He is wearing grey trousers as part of battledress. Known as 'overalls', they probably serve to keep his white pantaloons clean.

Riding costume (1798) with military inspired shako hat.

I thought Colonel Forster looked very becoming the other night at Sir William's in his regimentals.'

In *The Post-Captain* John Davis wrote: 'Women, like mackerel ... are caught with a red bait ... the blue jacket stands no chance.' It was not surprising that all the girls – and women – liked a man in uniform because most regiments in fact selected their recruits for their tall slim stature and youthful good looks. Some colonels actually found reason to discharge their veteran officers despite their obvious value in the melee because they wanted to replace them with younger more attractive men to improve the look of their regiment and therefore its prestige. Even so, Jane's loyalty remained with her brothers and William Price, who was 'complete in his lieutenant's uniform, looking and moving all the taller, firmer, and more graceful for it' in *Mansfield Park*.

Most found military glamour to be the height of chic; the towering shako hats, the gleaming gold braid, and flashing sword sent a clear message of indomitable strength. Many ladies in support of their officer beaux wore a feminised version of their uniforms with hussar jackets, pelisses, and Spencers with braid and frogging, whilst for civilian gentlemen there was an interchange of fashion from military to civilian dress and back. Pantaloons and Hessians became hugely popular at least partially because they were part of the heroic military image. Pantaloons were officially sanctioned for military campaigns in 1803, but even before that officers wore them at home – 'very proud of ourselves when at outquarters, we could thus dress, as it looked so like service'.

The Regency 'Buck' or 'Blood' so beloved of Pierce Egan was the bold, loud contrast to the waspish dandy. To the Buck, dress was only an adjunct to winning, whether racing horses, betting, or cards. They had also adapted the English country gentleman's look but their colours were brighter, their cut less artful, and their waistcoats were patterned. Their boots were allowed to get dirty and they would never dream of wearing the dress shoes and stirrup pantaloons that dandy Londoners had adopted for half dress.

The new style of male dressing certainly had its detractors – in 1803 the *General Evening Post* reports of a 'Brighton Blood' starting his day by 'endeavouring to give [himself] a slovenly appearance'. Jane was also less than enamoured: although Tom Bertram in *Mansfield Park* is something of a Buck his costume remains with the gentlemanly norm, but it is strident and odious John Thorpe in *Northanger Abbey* whom she characterises as:

> ...a stout young man, of middling height, who, with a plain face and ungraceful form seemed fearful of being too handsome, unless he wore the dress of a groom, and too much like a gentleman unless he were easy where he ought to be civil, and impudent where he might be allowed to be easy.

Left: Military inspired styles were very popular, like this *French Carriage Dress* (*La Belle Assemblée*, March 1818) adorned by military style braid 'frogging', the braid made into knots and loops to be used as fastenings.

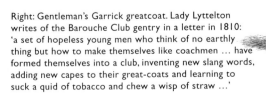

Right: Gentleman's Garrick greatcoat. Lady Lyttelton writes of the Barouche Club gentry in a letter in 1810: 'a set of hopeless young men who think of no earthly thing but how to make themselves like coachmen ... have formed themselves into a club, inventing new slang words, adding new capes to their great-coats and learning to suck a quid of tobacco and chew a wisp of straw ...'

ROUSSEAU AND FASHION AU NATUREL

ROUSSEAU'S PHILOSOPHIES had a particularly profound effect upon the lives of children. Prior to the publication of *Emile* in 1762, which extolled the child's right to freedom, childhood was considered to be at best an inconvenient preface to adulthood, and at worst an uncivilised state that had to be strictly controlled to avoid the inherent risks of original sin. Children were first tightly swaddled, then dressed identically in loose 'frocks' until, at around six years old, gender differences were acknowledged, when they would take on miniature versions of their parents' costumes.

Instead, in light of growing awareness of the links between health, hygiene and activity Rousseau advocated that:

> ...the limbs of a growing child should be free to move easily in his clothes; nothing should cramp their growth or movement; the French style of dress uncomfortable and unhealthy for a man, is especially bad for children ... the best plan is to keep children in frocks as long as possible and then to provide them with loose clothes, without trying to define the shape...Their defects of body and mind may all be traced to the same source, the desire to make men of them before their time.

His concept of childhood as a fleeting era of happiness and freedom to be enjoyed before it was all too quickly lost, struck a chord with the Romantic sensibilities of the time. Where children had previously only been painted as part of a family scene, they became the subject for portraits, their transient beauty captured, promising renewal for old dynasties, holding new hope for the future. Childhood began to be cherished, even emulated as sports and games became acceptable pastimes and the reforms in children's fashions began to influence adult fashions.

One of the first children to appear wearing a distinct child's outfit was John Charles Viscount Althrop, painted in 1786 at the age of four. He wears simple ankle-length trousers and a low-necked short jacket with an open shawl collar, in a plain buff fabric suitable for play. This ensemble with the

Opposite:
Sarah Barrett Moulin: Pinkie (Sir Thomas Lawrence, 1794). Although her muslin gown – very similar to Jane Austen's in *The Rice Portrait* (page 11) – is very much a girl's dress, it heralds the changes imminent in women's fashions.

The Graham Children (Hogarth, 1742) look beautiful but constrained in miniature versions of adult clothes – even the infant is wearing stays.

Master Henry Hoare as *The Young Gardener* (C. Wilkin after Sir Joshua Reynolds, c. 1789). Proving the virtue of the frock as a practical garment, he also wears shoes with latchets.

Boy in a Black Hat (Sir Joshua Reynolds, 1786). Viscount Althrop in one of the first outfits specifically for children, rather than for infants or scaled-down adult clothes.

Black Monday,
or *The Departure
for School*
(by John Jones
after W. R. Bigg,
1790). The little
boy in his skeleton
suit is less than
pleased at the
prospect of a new
term, although his
older brother in
his Eton Suit
appears more
stoical.

trousers buttoned onto the jacket just above the waist became the 'skeleton suit' and the staple of a little boy's wardrobe until the late 1830s, when it began to be superseded by the sailor suit. 'Breeching', the term used for the 'promotion' from frock to breeches, was a key transitional moment in a boy's life and keenly anticipated by relatives as it was the first step towards manhood, marking that he had successfully passed his formative years when at the greatest risk of infant mortality. In 1801 Jane writes to ask for the pattern of 'the jacket and trousers or whatever it is that Elizabeth's boys wear when they are first put into breeches'.

Older boys were reluctant to give up the comfort of trousers for the more restrictive breeches and from the skeleton suit came the trousers and short jacket combination that, with a plain linen collar added in about 1820 became the Eton suit. A more comfortable and active childhood did nothing to encourage young men to don the stuffy breeches and stockings of their fathers, and just as the young men of the jazz age would do a century later, they set their own styles.

There were fewer changes for girls. They were not emancipated from their infant frocks into adulthood through an equivalent to 'breeching' because they were never expected to be emancipated at all – not even by Rousseau. He had almost completely neglected

Morning
employments.
Needlework was
an important
forum for self-
expression for
young ladies
frequently denied
an adequate
education.

Fashion plate from a ladies' pocket book for 1795 showing the similarity between the women's slim muslin gowns and the child's frock. Both ladies wear the towering plumes so popular in the 1790s; the lady on the right wears a Mameluke cap like that which Jane borrowed in 1799.

women in his philosophies, and they were the only group for whom he did not advocate freedom. It was lamentably clear to Jane that even though the world was changing with unprecedented rapidity, it was doing so without women. As she acknowledges in *Emma*, schools for girls were little more than places 'where young ladies for enormous pay might be screwed out of health and into vanity'. Education was almost entirely geared towards teaching girls 'accomplishments' such as dancing or playing the harp that would display their prettiness and grace to the greatest advantage.

Muslin gowns, c. 1800–10 with cream embroidery of roses and foliage, and c. 1820 with all-over leaf pattern and gathered empire line bust. With gowns so sheer underwear really was a necessity!

With its low neck-line, small puffed sleeves and high waist with sash, the infant frock persisted with girls into later childhood and quite literally became the model for women's gowns during the first decade of the nineteenth century with the bodice *à l'enfant* with its rounded neckline with a running drawstring *en coulisse*. Sashes were an important accessory to young girls and in *Mansfield Park* Fanny Price fears that her cousins 'could not but hold her cheap when they found she had but two sashes and had never learned French.' The sweet prettiness and simplicity of these fresh, mainly white muslin gowns embodied the spirit of youthful freedom, but only if that freedom asked nothing more than to walk awhile gathering posies.

The one freedom women did gain was release from their corsets. Because of the natural ideal of allowing the body to display its given shape, caricatures usually portray women of the turn of the century as without underwear. The tight lacing of the eighteenth century giving a small natural waistline was gone, but stays did not disappear entirely for long when it was realised that some natural shapes are more desirable than others. Instead, stays were looser or concentrated higher at the artificial waistline below the bosom.

At this point stays still had shoulder straps, and in September 1813 Jane was 'really glad to hear that they are not to be worn so much off the shoulders as they were', and was pleased to note that 'the stays now are not made to force the bosom up at all; – that was a very unbecoming, unnatural fashion.' She may well have been referring to a 'divorce' – a punning name for a new corset that kept the breasts separate and according to *The Mirror of the Graces* in 1811 'made a sort of fleshy shelf, disgusting to the beholder'.

Whilst gowns had the extra weight of a train at the back they retained more modesty, but when the train became less fashionable there could be problems with the buttocks being visible or – horror of horrors – with the delicate fabric becoming caught between them! The answer was the 'invisible petticoat', which was a tube of flesh-coloured knitted stockinette worn tight around the legs. It restricted walking to tiny steps but allowed the gown to fall smoothly without any unsightly shadows of what lay beneath.

There was a move to introduce drawers but despite the obvious practicality, this was vehemently resisted because they were associated with women of low virtue, prostitutes or dancers who had been obliged to

The Stays ('The Progress of the Toilet', Gillray, c. 1810). 'Her bosom, which Nature planted at the bottom of her chest, is pushed up by means of wadding and whalebone to a station so near her chin that in a very full subject that feature is sometimes lost between the invading mounds.' (The *Morning Herald*, c. 1790s.)

The Graces in a Storm (Gillray, c. 1810). Caricaturists of the day were fascinated by the sartorial accidents that could befall the fashionable lady and produced numerous prints where, betrayed by their finery, ladies revealed more than they wanted to.

wear flesh-coloured silk knit tights since the days of Louis XV. Riding habits offered more freedom, and after a few nasty accidents revealing more than anyone cared to see, the wisdom of wearing legging-like tights was accepted as an extra precaution when riding.

In 1804 the *Chester Chronicle* noted that 'drawers of light pink [are] now the ton among our darling belles', but many women resisted wearing them until much later. They were adopted by Parisian ladies after the French Revolution, whose Grecian gowns were so accurate that the diaphanous fabric was barely joined at the sides, frequently opening to reveal the legs. Few English ladies went so far, but they too had moments of near nudity. *The Times* wrote:

> If the present fashion of nudity continues its career, the Milliners must give way to the Carvers, and the most elegant *fig-leaves* will be all the mode. The fashion for *false bosoms* has at least this utility, that it compels our fashionable fair to wear *something*.

Despite the call for all things au naturel, there were various falsies available to embellish nature's gifts. To wax lyrical about wax bosoms *The Oracle* wrote in 1800:

> Spite of the gibes of wanton wit,
> What emblems can the fair,
> Of their dear tender hearts more fit

Than waxen bosoms wear?
'Twixt mounts of wax and hills of snow
How small the difference felt!
With due degrees of heat we know
That both will gently melt.

These 'bosom friends' had to be fitted, and a description in *The True Briton* in 1800 recorded how a father was horrified when returning home he found a very smart young man with his hands all over his fourteen-year-old daughter, only to be told by his wife, 'the man is only fitting Euphrasia with a proper bosom; the girl cannot appear in fashionable company with her present horrid flatness of chest.'

Stockings did not climb much above the knee and were secured beneath it with garters, sometimes knitted, like those Jane Fairfax made for her grandmother in *Emma*. Garters were usually ribbons tied or buckled, but by the end of the eighteenth century, dentist Martin Van Butchell invented the 'spring garter' using the springs he had developed for false teeth, but they were expensive at 30 shillings a pair.

Jane was particular about her stockings, writing in October 1800, 'I like the stockings also very much, and greatly prefer having two pair only of that quality to three of an inferior sort'. In 1811 she bought silk stockings for 12 shillings a pair at the fashionable London store Grafton House and wrote that she was pleased with them despite the indignity of having to wait half an hour to be served. The quality of cotton stockings was hugely improved by developments in industrial processes (especially Arkwright's machines, which allowed for cotton to be spun extremely finely) and by 1822 fine cotton stockings were universal except for wear with silk gowns. W. Gardiner recalled in 1838 in the first volume of *Music and Friends* that 'No articles were so highly esteemed as English ladies' cotton stockings. Their peculiar whiteness and fineness recommended them as preferable to silk, and they sold for higher prices.' The Empress Josephine insisted that her stockings were ordered from England despite the war.

Good-Bye Till This Evening (La Mésangère c.1800). Visible beneath her raised skirt are her delicate slippers and white stockings with embroidered clocks at the ankle.

Le Bon Genre,
c.1810. Emma
is told in
The Watsons,
'nothing sets off
a neat ankle more
than a half boot;
Nankin galoshed
with black looks
very well'. She
replied that 'unless
they are so stout
as to injure their
beauty, they are
not fit for Country
walking.'

Ladies wore stockings with decorative embroidered clocks at their ankles, which in response to the ballet slipper style shoe became larger, decorating the instep within the 'V' of the low front of the shoe. Lace inserts were added to the clocks, which were embroidered around by the process of 'chevening' – a form of subtle embroidery – sometimes using contrasting colours to create designs often featuring crowns, trees or flowers.

Stockings were usually white or black for mourning, but colours were beginning to appear, as the *Chester Chronicle* reports with some disapproval in 1803: 'the only sign of modesty in the present dress of the ladies is the pink dye in their stockings, which makes their legs appear to blush for the total absence of petticoats'. Stockings worn with walking dresses were usually of a heavier weight and from 1802 appeared in brown, grey, or olive with yellow clocks.

Gentlemen largely wore tall military style boots for day and casual wear, but for 'full dress' occasions shoes were worn with white silk stockings with decorative clocks. These now had latchets to be laced over the instep with two pairs of holes, but were often made of delicate kid leather and very low cut. Little boys' shoes followed suit being increasingly low cut to become very similar to the ballet-slipper style shoes of their sisters and mothers.

Women's shoes came in a variety of fabrics as well as leather and were often made to match a particular gown. Many colours were available, usually pastel. In October 1800 Jane had new shoes: 'The pink shoes are not particularly beautiful, but they fit me very well', and in *Sanditon* Mr Parker exclaims: 'Blue Shoes and Nankin boots! …There was no blue Shoe when we passed this way a month ago … Glorious indeed!' Boots ranged from ankle to mid-calf and were frequently made of satin or kid leather but Nankin boots were made from a tough yellowy-brown cotton fabric, with a galosh section of black leather around the base of the foot, joined to the sole to keep the damp and mud out.

In the 1790s shoes with pointed toes and little heels were popular; some from Italy were almost as slender as stilettos. Heels rarely exceeded 2 inches in the arched wedge and were lower in the true wedge, but had dwindled to nothing by the 1820s. Most had some form of additional decoration – ruching, lace, or a pierced design to reveal a contrasting colour beneath. These were known as sandals, as were those that laced with ribbons that tied around the ankle, ballerina style.

'Straights' had been worn by both genders since the advent of the heel in 1600, but with the return to virtually flat shoes it was easier to make designated lefts and rights. Men – especially those with military duties – were eager to adopt them, but women were less keen because, as straights were alternated between the feet each time they were worn, they kept a nice symmetrical look. For a lady a dainty small foot was an asset, especially once the waltz became popular in 1816 and hems began to rise.

Shoe making was also a popular pastime: 'there was hardly a lady's work table that was not covered in shoemaker's tools', the Hon Mrs Calvert noted in her *Souvenirs* for 1808. 'I begin a new science today – shoemaking. It is all the fashion. I had a master with me for two hours.' And as Jane wrote to Anna her niece in 1814, 'your Grandmamma desires me to say that she will have finished your Shoes tomorrow & thinks they will look very well.'

Blue silk embroidered shoes and reticule, c. 1790s. The pretty netted and embroidered reticule with matching blue silk shoes came from the estate of Jane's brother Edward Austen Knight but it is unknown if they were worn by Jane or were embroidered by her for another family member.

45

RETICULE AND RIDICULE

SLENDER DIAPHANOUS DRESSES meant that there was now nowhere for pockets, and the 'reticule' – or 'ridicule' as it was christened by the satirists – was born along with a coterie of new accessories. These details added interest to a simple gown and their exotic nature spoke of the wealth, connections and taste necessary to procure them, whilst the delicate movements necessary to handle them helped to display a woman's pretty plump arms and dainty hands.

At most points in the preceding centuries skirts had been capacious enough to be able to accommodate small bags or separate 'pockets' tucked away within the folds, but the slender lines and diaphanous muslins of the 1800s rendered them redundant. Clearly ladies could not simply carry their possessions, and on the suggestion that Athenian ladies had once transported their possessions in small decorative bags, the reticule became the 'must have' accessory of 1800.

Muffs had grown in size when gowns grew narrower as though the soft bulk of a fur or swansdown muff drew favourable comparison to the slender silhouette. White swansdown was de rigueur for evening, whilst richer and warmer fur or sealskin would match fur-trimmed pelisses and cloaks by day. The capacious size made them handy for concealing private items like billets-doux, and it is likely that they were used to carry various personal items even if not sanctioned to do so.

The natural antecedent to the reticule was the knotting bag which, ostensibly to carry the accoutrements for the fashionable hobby, became something of a display item in the 1790s. It provided a pretty showcase for the ladies' knotting and needlework talents – which Mr Bingley in *Pride and Prejudice* considered a great female accomplishment – and as Lady Mary Coke noted as early as 1769: 'she had a knotting-bag, embroidered, hanging to her arm – "tho indeed" said she "I never knott, but the bag is convenient for one's gloves and Fan."'

In 1799 *The Times* reported 'the total abjuration of the female pocket... every fashionable fair carries her purse in her work-bag'. With the addition

Opposite:
The beautiful Madame Recamier (Francois Gerard, c. 1800) using her expensive shawl to add luxury and sensuality to a very simple muslin gown. Fashionable ladies were spoken of as being 'well draped' rather than well dressed, and in Paris there were those like Madame Gardel, performer of the shawl dance, who would give instruction in the graces of the shawl.

White silk reticule with border embroidered with floral designs and silver spangles, and tassels on each point (c. 1790–1810).

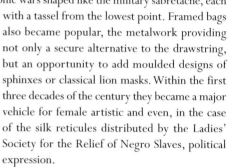

Eliza Farren, Countess of Derby (after Sir Thomas Lawrence, c. 1792) wearing a fur-trimmed cloak with large matching muff.

of longer handles and having been renamed 'indispensables', reticules were also featured in November that year in a fashion plate in *The Gallery of Fashion*. In France the knotting association was immortalised in the name, derived from *reticulum* (the Latin for 'net'). 'Reticule' took over as the fashionable name probably because of the glamorous classical motifs of the Parisian reticules made of cardboard or lacquered tin in the shape of Grecian urns suitable for the most elegant priestess.

Reticules could be bought from milliners ready made, but many ladies enjoyed making their own. In infinite variety reticules could match with a gown, Spencer, parasol, gloves or shoes. Usually in silk or, after 1810, increasingly in velvet, they were rectangular, lozenge shaped, or even during the Napoleonic wars shaped like the military sabretache, each with a tassel from the lowest point. Framed bags also became popular, the metalwork providing not only a secure alternative to the drawstring, but an opportunity to add moulded designs of sphinxes or classical lion masks. Within the first three decades of the century they became a major vehicle for female artistic and even, in the case of the silk reticules distributed by the Ladies' Society for the Relief of Negro Slaves, political expression.

The large picture hats of the 1790s gave way to a far less extravagant look. Hair became simple, close to the head and was often closely cropped in little curls decorated with a fillet or bandeau, or for evening, a simple spray of ostrich plumes. Without the need to balance on a large cushion of hair, hats took on a wide variety of styles, many closely fitted to the head.

Women also took on the fashion for tall crowned hats like the military shako. Hoods in various forms came in at the turn of the century as homage to the Grecian caul, a cloth or net that covered the hair in an elongated shape at the

'Promenade Dresses' (*Ackermann's Repository*, June 1811). Little face veils adorned a variety of hat styles and were thought a fashion essential by Mrs Elton in *Emma* who considered Emma's wedding *'extremely shabby, and very inferior to her own … very little white satin, very few lace veils; a most pitiful business!'*

back. There is an engraving of Jane's Aunt Perrot looking formidable in a dark silk hood.

Straw was very popular for morning or informal wear, and once a method of splitting straw was perfected, the English straw trade rose successfully to the challenge of replacing the delicate Italian leghorn straw that had been embargoed during the wars with France. Smarter afternoon and promenade hats were of fabrics shaped with wire, and evening styles were silk.

Little could seem more feminine than the bonnet, but the close-fitting style was originally masculine, based on a military helmet.

The *casquet à la Minerve* (*Le Bon Genre*, 1810).

49

'Walking Dress'
(*La Belle Assemblée*
May 1813). 'Short
dress of jacconet
muslin… Over this
our fair
pedestrians throw
a sky-blue scarf.
Bonnet of white-
willow shavings,
with a flower and
wreath of sky-blue.
Gloves and sandals
of sky-blue kid.
Necklace and
earrings of white
cornelian. Johnston
parasol. This
elegant appendage
to the walking
costume, is also of
sky-blue silk, and
finished with a rich
and deep fringe; it
has very recently
made its
appearance, and is
already a general
favorite.'

The *casquet à la Minerve* first appeared in the opera *La Caravanne du Caire* in 1797. It was a helmet of black velvet trimmed with a laurel wreath and ostrich plumes, and created a segue between the Egyptian influence and the coal-scuttle bonnet.

The 1790s also saw the rise of the 'oriental' style of a silk turban topped with nodding ostrich plumes. Jane borrowed a Marmalouc (or Mameluke) cap, which was 'all the fashion now' in January 1799. It was inspired by the success of Nelson's Nile Campaign in 1798, and a Nelson cap in Coquelicot

The Hats of 1810
(Haller von
Hallerstein, 1810).
The bonnet brim
grew exponentially
until 1810 when
the ladies who
wore them were
satirised as
'invisibles'. The
central lady also
carries an
oversized trefoil
fan.

velvet was one of the many articles of Nelsoniana worn to commemorate the hero.

Although it was beyond the range of most ladies to construct a hat, they delighted in trimming and re-trimming them to emulate the latest styles. A vogue for artificial flowers and fruits appeared in the late 1790s. In a letter to Cassandra Jane wrote:

Flowers are very much worn, & Fruit is still more the thing. – Elizth has a bunch of Strawberries, & I have seen Grapes, cherries, Plumbs, & Apricots – There are likewise Almonds & raisins, French plumbs & Tamarinds at the Grocers, but I have never seen any of them in hats'

In her next letter she adds 'besides I cannot help thinking that it is more natural to have flowers grow out of the head than fruit. Caps were frequently worn indoors, especially by older married ladies and Jane was very fond of wearing one even when only twenty-three. Her niece Caroline recalled:

She always wore a cap – Such was the custom with ladies who were not quite young – at least of a morning – but I never saw her without one, to the best of my remembrance either morning or evening.

'Half Dress'
(Ackermann's
Repository, January
1820). A veritable
fruit bowl of a hat
worn with a fawn
silk gown and
tucker.

In December 1798 when Jane is deeply involved in making a new cap, she writes to Cassandra:

> I took the liberty a few days ago of asking your black velvet bonnet to lend me its cawl, which it very readily did, and by which I have been enabled to give a considerable improvement of dignity to my cap, which was before too nidgetty to please me. I shall wear it on Thursday, but I hope you will not be offended with me for following your advice as to its ornaments only in part. I still venture to retain the narrow silver round it, Put twice round without any bow, and instead of the black military feather shall put in the Coquelicot one, as being smarter; and besides Coquelicot is to be all the fashion this winter. After the ball, I shall probably make it entirely black…

Scanty gowns were frequently chilly and a Spencer – far less popular in Europe where the fur trimmed Hussar jacket was preferred – was not always the answer especially with evening dress. The shawl provided an elegant way to add a little warmth without disguising the line of the gown or the figure beneath. First seen in London in around 1786, the shawl captured the imagination and remained popular in various forms for over a century.

'Morning Dress' (*Ackermann's Repository*, 1819). Jane always wore a cap 'as they save me a world of torment as to hair-dressing'.

Draping the shawl fittingly in the style of a classical statue was an art that reflected innate good taste and had the advantage of providing a frame for the most appealing assets whilst drawing a veil over those less attractive. But the shawl was not always praised: in 1806 *La Belle Assemblée* wrote, 'it is wonderful that the shawl should ever have found its path to fashionable adoption… it turns any female not beautiful and elegant into an absolute dowdy. It is the very contrast to the flowing Grecian costume …'

The Parasol became increasingly popular, not only for its exotic 'oriental' status but for practical reasons. As it became fashionable for ladies to spend more time outdoors the parasol became essential to preserve their pale complexions from strong sunlight. Silk parasols came in pretty pastel shades to complement the outfit or matching the colour of the reticule. The pagoda parasol was very fashionable with the fabric extended in a point towards the ferrule so that when open they had an elegant curved shape, and they were often enhanced by a knotted fringe. The fan or marquise parasol was also seen, its stem hinged so that the somewhat flatter fabric or paper leaf could be used as a vertical screen.

Umbrellas – most often green – were becoming useful especially as part of spa dress where the usual foul weather expedient of taking a sedan wasn't an option because walking was an obligatory part of the cure. In *Persuasion* Captain Wentworth refers to his umbrella when he tells Anne Elliot, 'I have equipped myself for Bath already.'

Always important status items, gloves remained usual for formal occasions for both men and women, who were admonished to wear them in church and at the theatre, but 'ladies should never dine with their gloves on – unless their hands are not fit to be seen.' Men would buy theirs from glove makers who would also provide their buckskin breeches. Made in beautiful quality leathers like doeskin or York tan, male styles were short, little beyond the wrist for all except riding gloves, and unobtrusive in neutral colours.

Throughout the eighteenth century women's gloves had usually been leather and supplied by a glove maker. But as gloves began to be made of fabrics complementary

Always an excellent needlewoman, Jane Austen worked this scarf in satin stitch on white muslin, c. 1800.

Madame Rivière (Ingres, 1805). In France the imported British cashmere shawls were heavily levied with taxes and on more than one occasion Napoleon in a fit of pique had whole shipments of shawls destroyed. Whatever her husband's political frustrations, it made no difference to Josephine: an inveterate shawl lover, she collected nearly four hundred, each costing 15–20,000 francs.

The Gallery of Fashion, 1796. The lady on the right demonstrates the vertical leaf of a marquise or 'fan' parasol.

The Coquette and Her Daughters (Debucourt, c. 1800). He is peeking at her prodigious bosom round the marquise parasol that he carries in the same hand as her pink reticule, whilst she carries a tiny fan.

to the outfit, increasingly they were bought from milliners. In the late 1790s there was a vogue for kid gloves printed with a variety of ingenious designs from elegant all over prints, to pretty hand painted designs such as a lady dressing a lamb with a garland of flowers. White was universal in the softest leathers including kid, chickenskin or limerick – the skin of unborn calves – which was reputed to make the wearer's hands and arms enviably white, clear, soft and smooth. Neutral shades of buff and stone, yellow, lilac and pastel shades were fashionable according to the colour of the gown. Black gloves were a statement of mourning until the 1820s when they became acceptable for fashionable wear in town.

'Promenade Dresses' (*Ackermann's Repository*, July 1810). Writing from Bath in May 1801, Jane observed, 'black gauze cloaks are worn as much as anything'. A similar effect could be achieved by netting, as Miss Tilney's friend Miss Andrews did in *Northanger Abbey*: 'she is netting, herself the sweetest cloak you can conceive'.

Generally elbow-length, longer gloves often had the problem of slipping and wrinkling. Glove strings first appeared in the 1780s; they were ribbons tied or sometimes fastened with a diamond buckle 'high over the elbow to preserve the arm in beauty for womanhood'. After Waterloo a new prudery dawned in reaction to the freedoms of the revolutionary period and gloves became extremely long, almost in compensation for the short puffed sleeves that were still de rigueur for evening.

Jane does not specify the length of them but she bought some 'light and pretty' coloured gloves for herself and Cassandra in May 1812 for 4 shillings, which must have been an exceptional bargain as she writes: 'everybody at chawton will be hoping & predicting that they cannot be good for anything, and their worth certainly remains to be proved, but I think they look very well.'

The fan was the essential evening accessory as well as being pretty; they were extremely practical at the assemblies, which with their increasing popularity were often tremendously crowded, hot and airless. More importantly, clever use of a fan could draw attention to the owner's beautiful eyes whilst concealing her pretty smile and, depicting classical, romantic, or

Mademoiselle Rivière (Ingres, c. 1804). Her exceptionally long suede fingerless gloves are fastened with glove strings and she wears a snake-style boa of white fox.

fashionable scenes, convey something of her innate taste and sophistication.

Fans, which had become an important accessory during the eighteenth century, remained so, but increasingly the hand-painted biblical or pastoral scenes were replaced by printed political messages. Political fans played their part in the French Revolution, spreading propaganda or concealing hidden messages of aristocratic support, and it was said that Charlotte Corday carried a fan in one hand as she plunged the knife into Marat.

In England a fan of 1789 was issued as a patriotic gesture in support of King George III after another bout of illness, 'On the King's Happy Recovery'. Fans celebrated Nelson's sea victories and followed each development in the war, giving details of the ships involved, those captured and sunk. Other fans were ivory or bone with incredibly intricate carving to look like muslin. There was a system of fan etiquette designating the correct ways to use and hold a fan to enhance the beauty and grace of the hands. There was also a language of the fan, probably derived from *The Speaking Fan* published by Charles Badini in 1797. Displaying the 'Rudiments of Fanology', it began as a party game but developed into a tool of romantic intrigue. However, it is for concealment that Catherine Morland uses her fan at the Cotillion Ball in *Northanger Abbey* when the boorish John Thorpe is in sight: 'that she might not appear to observe or expect him, she kept her eyes intently fixed on her fan.'

With the rise of the reticule, fans became smaller at the beginning of the nineteenth century, and those displaying images of the sights of the Grand Tour were particularly popular. English taste remained modest, with church fans printed with psalms, educational fans with maps or botanical diagrams, and art fans depicting famous works, although pierced ivory *brisé* fans remained most popular. Cockade fans that opened up into a full circle became popular from 1808, some including a spy glass in the centre, with crape fans embroidered with silver and spangles leading the fashion in 1817.

Jane refers to her white fan in her letters but ivory fans remained the most usual, possibly because they were also used as dance fans to make a note of the names of dance partners. This is most likely what William is doing 'working away his partner's fan as if for life' at the ball in *Mansfield Park*. Little jewellery was worn with the *style à l'anglaise* but watches began to be worn suspended from the waistline, men adding a fob

'Watering Place Morning Dress' (*The Gallery of Fashion*, October 1795). Pea green gloves, green silk handkerchief tied over the hat, green sash and shoes show that accessories could be used to quite striking effect to pull an outfit together.

Early nineteenth-century fans. Carved *brisé* fans were hugely popular, as were paper or silk fans with neoclassical motifs.

on the opposite side to create symmetry. The French Revolution caused many ladies to get rid of their jewels in a desperate attempt to avoid *la guillotine*, their diamonds replaced with neoclassical pearls, amethysts and cameos. These they wore literally from head to foot – from their classically inspired tiaras, golden girdles, and slave bangles to the rings on their toes.

Madame de Pompadour had carved her own cameos, but for those less talented and less wealthy Josiah Wedgewood created a method for making porcelain cameos. The passion for cameos inspired a flood of neoclassical jewellery that drew inspiration from all parts of the ancient world as dictated by the latest discoveries at Herculaneum, Pompeii, and after the Nile campaign, Egypt.

In 1800 the *Morning Post* declared amethyst and topaz to be 'preferable to all

'Carriage Dress' (*Ackermann's Repository*, January 1810). The ermine-trimmed cape and matching cap would be snug for travelling and the watch pinned at her elevated waistline would help her keep track of the time!

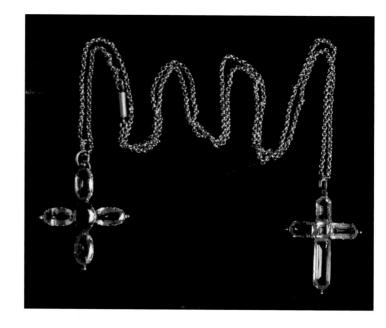

The topaz crosses given to Jane and Cassandra by their brother Charles.

others' for necklaces and earrings. It was perfect then, that in May 1801 Jane wrote to tell Cassandra that their brother Charles 'has been buying gold chains and topaze crosses for us; - he must be well scolded'. She must have been pleased because she commemorated the occasion by having Fanny Price receive a topaz cross from her brother William in similar circumstances. Unlike Charles, William did not supply a chain (at first Fanny wore the cross on a ribbon) but Mary Crawford gives her a gold chain 'prettily worked'. These gold chains made a less costly alternative to strings of pearls, which were fashionably draped between cameos at the girdle and bust-line.

In *La Nouvelle Héloïse*, Rousseau had glorified sentiment and virtue, and advocated sentimental jewellery over artificial finery, especially for day wear. There were brooches painted with ladies weeping over tombstones surrounded by willow trees, parures of ivy leaves and owls for remembrance, or snakes for eternity. Hair work was a more literal way of commemorating the departed, with bracelets or watch chains woven from the hair of the deceased, or strands to form entwined initials sealed under crystal. Only the most extreme wore one of their teeth as a tie pin!

Queen Louise Augusta of Prussia (Vigée Le Brun, 1802). In 1805 the *Journal des Dames* wrote: 'a fashionable lady wears cameos at her girdle, cameos in her necklace, cameos on each of her bracelets, a cameo on her tiara. The antique stones are more fashionable than ever, but in default of them one may employ engraved shells.'

AFTER THE AGE OF ELEGANCE

JANE AUSTEN visited Carlton House on 13 November 1815 when the Prince Regent gave her the honour of allowing her to dedicate her latest novel *Emma* to him. She must have given considerable thought to what she wore that day but unfortunately did not discuss it in her letters. The librarian of Carlton House, the Reverend James Stanier Clarke greeted her with due ceremony as a fellow author and gave her a tour of the Prince's extravagant home. It seems she made quite an impression on him as they struck up a relationship via letter. He also painted a watercolour of her in his 'Friendship Book' depicting her wearing a white muslin gown with a stole-like cloak of black with red, a matching hat of black velvet with red trim, red shoes and brown fur muff. Jane was less impressed, ambivalent about how she should dedicate the work, and very disapproving of the Prince's excessively lavish lifestyle, especially at a time when the country was plunged into recession.

Her thoughts would be echoed by many others before the end of the decade. The 'age of elegance' was slipping away; in 1816 Byron left England in disgrace, Beau Brummell fled to France to escape his debts, and Jane Austen became increasingly ill with what is thought to have been Addison's disease. The royal wedding on 2 May 1816 saw all hopes rest on Princess Charlotte, the plump and happy girl who pleased the nation by preferring only English gowns. She also enjoyed Jane's works, particularly *Sense and Sensibility*, saying:

> I think Maryanne & me are very like in disposition, that certainly I am not so good, the same imprudence, &c, however remain very like. I must say it interested me much.

Revolution had changed the world and fashion had dressed it accordingly. The war had been the main impetus for the last twenty-three years, introducing new ideas and new cultures, each reflected in what was worn. The textile industry had been affected exponentially, developing new processes to provide fashions that had formerly been imported, and to supply massive orders for military uniforms, but the cost to the workforce had been high.

Opposite: One of the greatest beauties of the age, Margaret, Countess of Blessington (Sir Thomas Lawrence, 1822).

Portrait of Jane Austen by the Reverend James Stanier Clarke from his 'Friendship Book' painted in 1815 after they met on her visit to Carlton House.

Despite proving England's pre-eminence, the post-Waterloo attitude was one of dour sobriety for all except the Prince's court. They partied on, unaffected by the small groups of heroes, once splendid, their red or blue now ragged, who were left begging by the roadside by the authorities who refused to pay the wages that were owed to them for years of service.

Aristocratic and genteel ladies set up societies to raise money for Waterloo widows and the Waterloo wounded, but gone were the days when beautiful political patrons would have been able to exert a little influence directly. Men and women were becoming polarised: once men had realised the comfort and camaraderie of their own company they were less keen to adopt the 'full dress' and fine manners necessary for female society. Women lost any freedoms they may have gained with the rise of evangelicalism and sentimentality, when it was remembered that women were 'inherently sinful' and the only way they could redeem themselves was through a life of modesty, sobriety, charity and silence.

Carlton House as it was in about 1808.

Men had chosen to make the Great Renunciation, giving up fine fabrics, decoration and even colour to create the convention of the business suit, but in exchange they gained a new world of business and industry crowned with a top hat. For women the renunciation was enforced by a strict moral opprobrium that stripped away the idealism that had been so carefully represented through dress, replacing it with a facile submissive prettiness. The waist was gradually restored to its natural position and laced tighter than ever, whilst further encumbrance was added as sleeves grew wider, hems gained width and heavy decoration, and bonnets became blinkers to the world.

Princess Charlotte of Wales in 1816 looking elegant in striped gown with luxurious Paisley shawl.

Below far left: 'Evening Dress for Mourning' (Ackermann's Repository, December 1817). The nation was plunged into mourning when Princess Charlotte died in childbirth on 6 November 1817. Mourning was observed for royalty as well as even the most distant family members, but the expense of buying special mourning clothes would sometimes mar the sentiment.

Left: Deep blue dress with ruff and shawl, 1819. The days of girlish freedom were over as women would soon have to cope with the enforced concealment of poke bonnets and an ever-narrowing waistline demanded by corsets even more cruel than their eighteenth-century predecessors.

INDEX

Page numbers in italics refer to illustrations